Route 66 Today
Chicago, Il. to Needles, Ca.

*Enjoy
Route 66
Ray Wolf*

Ray Wolf and John Donovan (below) are pictured here. They are about to depart Hope, Rhode Island, July 29, 2014, on a journey of a life time.

On the cover: This image is viewing a striking section of Old Route 66 wandering from Kingman, Arizona to Oatman, Arizona. From there the Mother Road then continues from Oatman to Needles, California.

Route 66 Today

Chicago, Il. to Needles, Ca.

Raymond A. Wolf

W O L F
PUBLISHING

Published by Wolf Publishing
Hope, Rhode Island

Printed in the United States of America

For all general information:
E-mail: theewolf@cox.net

For orders:

Visit us on the Internet at: www.raywolfbooks.com

To my mom,
Helen O. Larson,
whose poetry has inspired
my journey

Contents

Acknowledgments

First and foremost I desire to thank my wife Ramona for suggesting I find a partner to travel with. See page 134.

Second, I would like to thank my friend John Donovan, for deciding to take the trip down Route 66 with me. We had an absolutely wonderful experience. You are a great traveling partner.

Third, once more I want to thank my wife Ramona along with John's wife Mary. Without their encouragement and their assistance while we were gone, the trip would not have been possible.

Fourth, I want to give a great big thank you to Jennifer Carnevale again for editing my tenth book.

All images are from the author's collection unless otherwise noted.

Introduction

The year was 1925 and Cyrus Avery (1871-1962) was knee deep in meetings with a committee to create a route from Chicago to Los Angeles. After moving from his home state of Pennsylvania to Oklahoma he became the highway commissioner. He worked so diligently to make his dream come true that he soon became known as the "Father of Route 66". The idea was to link together existing roads from town to town. Most of which were the main street in each town. Therefore, the route picked up the title then and is still known as being "The Main Street of America".

By the end of 1925 it had been agreed the route would begin in Chicago, Illinois and travel through Missouri, Kansas, Oklahoma, Texas, New Mexico, Arizona and California, ending in Los Angeles. Later it was extended to the Santa Monica Wharf. Avery and his committee finally witnessed it being commissioned in November 1926.

In 1939 John Steinbeck (1902-1968) published a novel titled *The Grapes of Wrath,* of which he won a Pulitzer Prize. It was about the exodus of people escaping the dust bowl area during the Great Depression of the 1930s. In his novel he called Route 66 "The Mother Road" because it was leading these desperate folks to hopefully a better life in California, much like a mother would. This name for the road has also stuck to this day. Henry Fonda starred in the movie in 1940.

It is with great pleasure the author informs you that 80 to 85 per cent of Route 66 is still there and drivable. He also wishes to report to you the eight states it travels through are doing a magnificent job of signing it with the familiar brown Historic Route 66 signs.

As you travel through the pages of *Route 66 Today,* you will experience towns that have become ghost (see pages 56-57) when the Interstate by-passed them. Then further down the road you will encounter towns that are being revived. Buildings are being restored and businesses have new life as people from all over the world (see page 50) come to the United States just to travel the famous Route 66.

The following poem was written by the author's mother, Helen O. Larson when she was 80 years old. It is dedicated to the people that traveled Route 66 in the 1930s, escaping the dust bowl area and the Great Depression. Enjoy the trip you about take down *Route 66 Today*.

The Great Depression

Our country had a crisis many, many years ago
And how we survived it, I will never know

Many nights we went to bed hungry, hunger pains all night long
We don't know what happened to cause our country to go wrong

Soup kitchens sprung up all over, people could have soup once a day
It will be forever embedded in my memory to stay

My brother got a job shucking corn; the man paid ten cents an hour
So many times my mother wished she had a bag of flour

One day I found a crust of bread, my mother said to me
You break it right now and share it; your brothers are also hungry

No money for food or cloths or to see a movie show
How we got through the depression we will never know

We couldn't take a bus to pass away some time
The fare was only a nickel, just half a dime

Lucky we didn't get sick, a doctor we couldn't afford
Someone was watching over us, I'm sure it was the Lord

Then one day all that changed, an election took place
And Franklin Roosevelt ran and he won the race

All the mills started up and we got a raise right away
My friend came to me and said thirty-five cents an hour they'll pay

We were getting twenty-five cents an hour and now with the extra ten
We knew we would celebrate though we didn't know when

As I write this poem, dear God I ask you
Don't ever again let your people go through what we went through.

One

ILLINOIS

The Route 66 journey begins at the corner of Adams Street and Lake Shore Drive in downtown Chicago. However, it is a must to have breakfast at the famous Lou Mitchell's Restaurant and Bakery. With a full stomach and a full tank of gas let's begin.

When Route 66 was commissioned in 1926, Lou Mitchell's Restaurant and Bakery located in downtown Chicago had already been in business for three years. It is to be found at 565 W. Jackson Boulevard, the terminus of Route 66, now a one way street headed east. Therefore, one block North, Route 66 begins on Adams Street, a one way street headed west.

Lou Mitchell's was inducted into the Route 66 Hall of Fame on June 8, 2002. This year, 2015, they are proud to be celebrating their 92nd year in business.

Lou Mitchell's waitress, Tina Wolfe, (really) smiles for the camera with the authors traveling buddy, John Donovan. Pictured below is what the author received when he ordered one egg, bacon, and home fries with coffee. Tina explained they constantly beat the eggs to fluff them up. This is actually one egg and the only place to start a Route 66 journey.

Pictured here is the Castle Car Wash. A one of its kind design building erected in 1925 at 3801 W. Ogden Av. on Chicago's West Side. By the 1930s it was in the company of over twenty gas stations on Ogden Av.

This is Henry's 1950s Hot Dog stand in Chicago's suburb of Cicero at 6031 W. Ogden Av. It is a must stop place for anyone who likes hot dogs. The dining area is small but cozy and you order at the counter.

Dick's On 66 tow truck on the roof appears to be towing a car that was going to "California or Bust" but did not make it. The Ford "Car 54" with siren, light, and antenna is standing by to chase speeders in Joliet.

Across the street the Blues Brothers are in front of the sign on the roof stating; Joliet, Kix On 66. It is a Rich and Creamy ice cream stand. They also sell soft drinks. It states; Get Your Kicks With Route 66 (Root) Beer.

Wilmington is well known for this 20 foot fiberglass spaceman named Gemini Giant. He has stood quietly at 810 E. Baltimore Street inviting travelers to stop and come on in to the Launching Pad Drive-In for over 50 years.

The Launching Pad Drive-In, below, has a sign in the window stating; Sorry We Are Closed. Unfortunately, the sign in the window to the left announces it is For Sale.

The Polk-a-Dot Drive-In opened in Braidwood in 1956. Elvis stands on the side of Route 66 tempting motorists to stop and have a bite to eat. Inside you can visit with James Dean, Marilyn Monroe and Betty Boop.

During its heyday, Route 66 became a four lane highway in some areas. This section between Braidwood and Dwight has regressed back to the original two lane road.

Ambler's Texaco Gas Station was built in 1933. It later became Becker's Marathon Gas Station in Dwight and was the longest operating gas station on Route 66 when it closed in 1999. The blue sign above the Texaco gas pumps announces it is a "Route 66 Nostalgic Attraction". It was restored in '05-'07 then reopened in 2007 as a visitor center. John is seen inspecting a Marathon gas pump beside a restored fire engine.

This Standard Oil station was built in Odell in the 1930s. It later became a Phillips 66 and then a Sinclair station. Today, it has been restored by the citizens of Odell to be used as a visitor center for Route 66 travelers.

Bob Waldmire converted this school bus and traveled up and down the Mother Road. Along the way he became famous for his drawings and maps of Route 66. His father, Ed Waldmire Jr., ran the Cozy Dog Drive-In in Springfield from 1946 until his death in the early 1990s. Home to the famous corn-dog on a stick, it is now run by his daughter-in-law.

Brothers, Isaac and Absalom Funk arrived from Kentucky in 1824 and called the area Funk's Grove. Isaac amassed 25,000 acres and began raising cattle. In 1891 Isaac's grandson, Arthur Funk, opened the first commercial maple syrup camp. Today 7th generation Michael Funk and wife Debbi (above) run the maple syrup business and ship world-wide.

The Dixie Travel Plaza, aka Dixie Truck Stop and Dixie Trucker's Home is located in McLean. It opened in 1928 by J.P. Walters and John Geske. By 1930 it was extended into a full size restaurant. It only closed one day in 1965 due to a fire. The building has been expanded many times.

The tomb of Abraham Lincoln is in Oak Ridge Cemetery in Springfield. The burial vault is located in the rear of the monument and is 30 inches behind a reddish marble block and 10 feet below the floor. The 117 foot obelisk stands on a rectangular base and was built 1868-74, three years after Lincoln was assassinated in 1865. Below is a replica of the statue in the Lincoln Memorial in Washington, D.C. Entombed here with him is his wife, Mary Todd Lincoln, and three of their four sons.

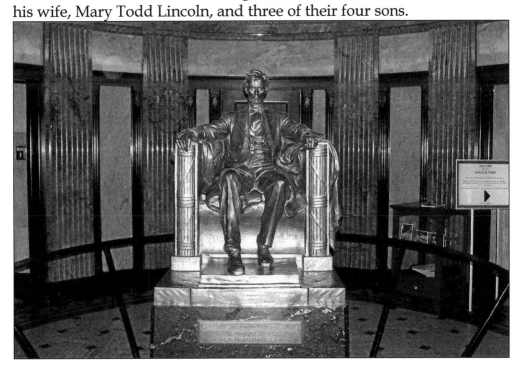

This very bumpy original pavement of Route 66 is encountered south of Springfield on the way to Gillespie.

The "Main Street of America" travels down the Main Street of Gillespie. At the height of 66 travelers, traffic was bumper to bumper every day.

Two

MISSOURI

As Route 66 crosses into Missouri the journey continues. It used to be that traffic on Old Route 66 would cross the Missouri River on the spectacular Chain of Rocks Bridge. Today the beltway, Interstate 270, and Interstate 64 carries the traffic to St. Louis.

Below the surface of the Mississippi River there is an unseen chain of rocks, hence the Chain of Rocks Bridge. Construction started on the 40 foot wide, mile long bridge in 1927 and opened to traffic in 1929. It was replaced in 1968 by the new Chain of Rocks Bridge carrying I-270, just 2,000 feet upstream. After lying dormant many years, it opened in 1999 as part of the Rt. 66 Bikeway and is part of the 300 mile Trailnet system.

The five bridge trusses that make up this bridge rest 60 feet above the Mississippi River on huge concrete piers. The 30 degree bend mid-way made it very difficult for traffic to maneuver as trucks became larger.

Meramec Caverns in Stanton have been the site of tours since 1933. The story goes that Jesse James and his gang used the caverns as a hideout.

The Wagon Wheel Motel in Cuba is the oldest continuously operated motel on Route 66. It has been completely restored. Connie's Shoppe and motel office is located out front in the large building seen below. A 1950 Chevrolet is parked beside the Standard Oil Products office. The original gas pumps proudly stand guard out front.

Four miles west of Cuba is the Fanning 66 Outpost general store. Beside all the Rt. 66 merchandise, they also have an Archery Pro Shop with 3 target ranges. They also have the World's Largest Rocking Chair. It was erected on April 1, 2008 and certified by Guinness World Records on September 4, 2008. It stands 42'-1" tall, 20'-3" wide and weighs 26,500 lbs. It was designed by John R. Bland and fabricated by Joe Medwick.

This is one of many steel bridges encountered on Route 66. Mr. Munger started a barbecue place located on the Big Piney River in the 1930-40s. When he passed away his wife married Emmett Moss, hence it became the Monger Moss Sandwich Shop. In 1946 the Munger Moss Motel was built. Over the years it has been expanded, like in 1961 when 26 rooms were added. Today Route 66 travelers have made it a thriving business, owned and operated by Bob and Ramona Lehman for the last 30 years.

This steel bridge crosses the Little Piney River. There is a marker on the side of the road that states on March 29, 2009 there was record flooding. The river actually flowed right over the road bed of the bridge.

Just outside of Joplin is this building that never saw completion. It appears it was to be a commercial enterprise, what with the two large windows in front. However, it sets quite a distance off the road.

This is one of many stunning sunsets to be seen on Route 66. This one is captured in the rear view mirror while parked in a camp ground at the end of another very long and exhilarating day.

Three

KANSAS

Route 66 cuts across the southeast corner of Kansas for only 12.8 miles. It was the first of the eight states that Route 66 passed through to be completely paved. However, Kansas was also the only state to be completely bypassed when Interstate 44 (I-44) was opened in 1961.

Heading west on route 66, this sign welcomes you to Galena, the first town in Kansas. It is only two miles from the border of Missouri.

This photograph shows Route 66 traveling through the business center of Galena. Kansas completed concreting their portion of Rt. 66 in 1929.

Just outside of Galena rests this well used and rusty Erie Lackawanna diesel locomotive. Considering the track does not extend in front of or behind (below) the companion rusty caboose; it looks like they will be here for quite some time. They both have seen better days. It almost appears they are on display.

The old MKT line (Missouri, Kansas, Texas) Galena Train Depot has been completely restored into the Galena Mining & Historical Museum. A huge storage area can be seen to the left at the rear of the building.

The author is pictured here August 15, 2014 with Joe Douffet, a volunteer, along with his wife Wilma, who helps keep the visitor center operating. Joe and Wilma have been married 62 years.

Each morning Joe drives a different one of the antiques out of the back storage area and displays it in front of the depot, alongside Route 66.

Galena likes to welcome visitors to their town with this beautiful post card mural on the side of a building. They are proud to be on Route 66.

Rainbow Curve Bridge was constructed in 1929 over Brush Creek. It is the only survivor of the three original Marsh Arch Bridges on Route 66. It was listed on the National Registry March 10, 1983.

The visitor center in this restored old Phillip's 66 gas station is the last one on Kansas Route 66 before entering Oklahoma.

34

Four

OKLAHOMA

Route 66, The Mother Road, travels over 400 miles in Oklahoma, more miles than any of the other seven states. Oklahoma is proud to affirm they have the title of having the longest drivable stretch of The Main Street of America.

This original Marathon Gas Station is now a Dairy King and sells soft whipped ice cream. It also advertises: One and Only "Route 66 Cookies" Sold Anywhere. It is located in Commerce.

This Conoco station looks like it was an afterthought, being attached to the large building. The sign between two pumps announces a gas war.

This Oklahoma monument states: Historic Route 66 Ribbon Road or Sidewalk Highway. Completed in 1922 as Federal Highway Project No. 8. Running 15.46 miles from Miami to Afton. The only remaining 9 foot section of original pavement on the old Route 66 system, taken out of service in 1937. A National Register of Historic Places Site.

It was called the Sidewalk Highway or Ribbon Road because it was only wide enough for one vehicle at a time. Each motorist would steer their right wheels onto the dirt shoulder until they passed each other.

The Avon Court, opened in Afton in 1936, has seen better days. When Interstate 44 bypassed them in 1957 it lured traffic away from Route 66. Many local businesses did not survive. Only three of the seven are left.

This is the original roadbed and bridge that crossed the Little Cabin Creek. Route 66 now follows the adjacent highway; Routes 60 and 69.

Two forlorn 1959 Edsel Villager nine passenger station wagons sit along Route 66 in White Oak.

Hugh Davis built this 80 foot Blue Whale in the 1970s as an anniversary gift for his wife Zelta. It is on Spunky Creek just east of Catoosa on 66.

Evangelist Oral Roberts founded the Oral Roberts University (ORU) in Tulsa in 1963. Today enrollment is over 3,000 and in 2012 was ranked one of the Best in the West by The Princeton Review. The praying hands on the facing page are to the right of this impressive entrance to the university. However, originally the hands were across the street (see page 42) in front of three other buildings Roberts built from 1978-81. He called them The City of Faith. It consisted of one 20 story research center, one 30 story hospital, and one 60 story clinic. It never was to be what Oral Roberts dreamed of. Occupancy was so low it closed in 1989. The Praying Hands were moved to ORU in 1991. Today the complex has been renamed the Cityplex Towers and is mostly used for office space.

This 60 foot 30 ton bronze sculpture entitled Praying Hands represents the hands of science and faith together in prayer. It was originally at the entrance of the hospital across the street. See next page.

The City of Faith Medical and Research Center in Tulsa was the second tallest building in Oklahoma at the time. Opened in 1981, it closed 1989.

City of Faith

As I saw the beautiful City of Faith
Descending from the sky
I was over-come by emotion
And with joy I started to cry

All nations would come to the city
The halt, the lame, the blind
It's such a beautiful city
And the only one of its kind

A city where people can pray
Their sicknesses all will be healed
And the doctors and nurses there
Will be the best in their field

And the beautiful hands in the foreground
Reaching up toward the sky
Giving hope and faith to the sick
They'll be healed, they won't have to die

And the River of Life at the entrance
With its water so crystal clear
Is a reminder to us all
That healing hands are here

And the Trees of Life so pretty
In front of the buildings so tall
Spreading their lovely branches
Giving faith and hope to all

Written by Helen O. Larson

1982 – Age 71

About the City of Faith in Tulsa, Oklahoma

Construction began on the Rock Café in Stroud in 1936. Roy Rieves paid $100 for the land and $5 for the local sandstone left over from the building of Route 66 in 1926. Betsy the grill, used since 1939 when the café opened, survived a devastating fire in May 2008. The building was totally rebuilt in 2009 with Betsy in full service again. Present proprietor Dawn Welch is the basis for the character Sally in the Pixar film Cars.

This photograph depicts the Lincoln Motel on Route 66 in Chandler. It also shows how well maintained the property appears.

The Route 66 Interpretive Center along with the Oklahoma Route 66 Association is housed in The Old Chandler Armory. It was built in 1936 by the Works Progress Administration (WPA). The outer walls are 20 inches thick and chiseled by hand. A new armory was built in 1971.

This quaint little Phillips 66 filling station in Chandler was built in 1930. Bill Fernau bought it in 1999 and is totally restoring it to original status. In 2002 he was awarded the Cyrus Avery Award for preservation.

Pioneer merchant A.E. Mascho built these two Sandstone buildings in 1897. They are now the oldest buildings in Lincoln County and are used by the Lincoln County Historical Society and Pioneer Museum. The first floor houses the old fashioned general store. The old post office and telephone switchboard is included. The second floor features the living quarters used by residents who owned or operated the store.

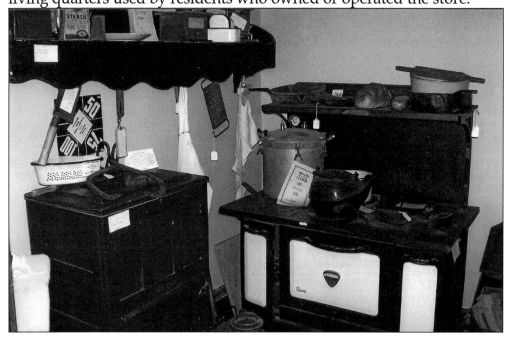

Among the rooms on the second floor is the kitchen (facing page) with a box of starch on the shelf. The good old rolling pin rests on the stove. On top of the ice box (before refrigerators) is a pair of ice tongs. Above, is a typical frontier bedroom with a handmade quilt covering the bed. Below, is a little girls' room complete with games, dolls and a carriage.

This monument reads: Rt 66 Whether motorists called it The Ozark Trail, The Will Rogers Highway, Main Street of America or the Mother Road, everyone remembers Arcadia's Round Barn. The well known landmark was built in 1898 by William Harrison Odor. After the route was designated a national highway in 1926, improvements were made to the 1917 roadbed. The original road between Edmond and Arcadia was constructed by convict labor. The highway through Arcadia was paved in 1929.

After renovations it was opened on April 4, 1992.

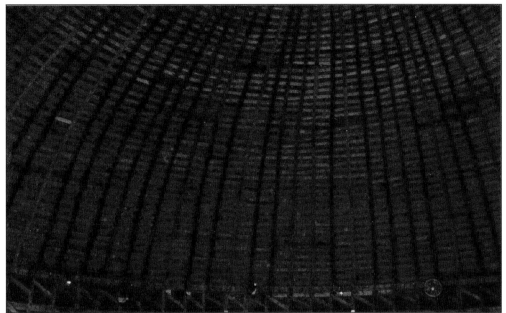

The barn was built from locally grown burr oak. It stands 43 feet high with a diameter of 60 feet. The first floor sheltered the animals while the loft was originally intended for hay and grain. However, the loft was also used for dances and concerts. By the 1980s it had fallen into serious disrepair. Restoration began in 1988 and took four years. (See page 48.) These two photographs show the complexity of the roof construction. The author met a mother and teenage daughter from Bonn, Germany. They had come to the United States on vacation just to travel Route 66.

This Seaba DX Station was built in 1921 by John and Alice Seaba. This was five years before Route 66 was certified. After a number of owners, Jerry Reis and Gerald Tims bought the building in 2007. They have restored the building to its original appearance and have opened Seaba Station Motorcycle Museum in Warwick. This couple from Basque, Spain spoke very little English however, was enjoying traveling Rt. 66.

This well maintained steel bridge is outside Bethany. Below, this sign indicates that nine miles down a side road is the grave site of Jesse Chisholm. He first marked the famous Chisholm Trail in 1864. From 1867 to 1872 more than three million head of Texas longhorn cattle were driven up the Chisholm Trail from Texas to the R.R. in Abilene, Kansas.

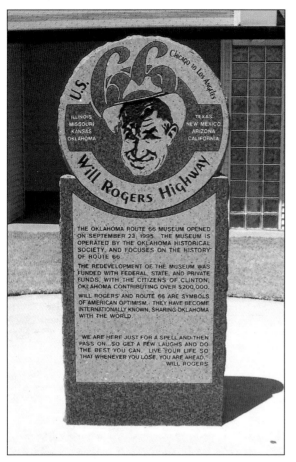

This monument reads: The Oklahoma Rt. 66 Museum opened September 23, 1995. The museum is operated by the Oklahoma Historical Society and focuses on the history of Route 66. The redevelopment of the museum was funded by federal, state and private funds, with the citizens of Clinton contributing over $200,000. Will Rogers and Route 66 are symbols of American optimism. They have become internationally known, sharing Oklahoma with the world.

This diner was relocated to the Route 66 Museum property in Clinton. Will Rogers said; "We are here for just a spell and then pass on...so get a few laughs and do the best you can. Live your life so that whenever you lose, you are ahead."

This 1962 Impala SS is in the window of the Route 66 Museum. It can also be seen in the window of the photograph on the opposite page.

The Glancy Motor Hotel is located at 217 E. Gary Boulevard in Clinton. Pop Hicks Restaurant next door was built in 1936. It is sad to report it burnt down in 1999. Another Route 66 icon has disappeared.

Traveling on old Route 66 is a little slower than the super highway of Interstate 40 running parallel to it. This stretch is outside of Clinton.

Pictured here is another abandoned building found along Route 66. This one is just outside of Elk City.

Even though 80 to 85% of Route 66 is drivable and very well signed, occasionally there are sections that are long forgotten and impassable.

Between Erick, Oklahoma and Shamrock, Texas lays Texola, the last town in Oklahoma. This photograph shows the approach to the town. It was originally settled in the early 1900s as Texokla and Texoma. Texola's population grew rapidly in the 1920s with the development of Route 66. By the 1930 census it had grew to 581 residents. When Interstate 40 opened to the north in 1975, population began to decrease. The 2010 census stated there were 36 hearty souls still living there.

The house pictured on the previous page along with the two pictured here is what most of the town has regressed to. It is close to being a true ghost town. As the older folks pass on, their property begins the process of looking like these abandoned homes. The population has been steadily declining since the 1930 census with no signs of changing.

At the edge of town, just before entering Texas, there is one business in Texola. It is the Tumbleweed Grill and Waterhole #2 Country Store. The Grill is a full service restaurant serving breakfast, lunch and dinner. The country store can supply your needs to continue the journey down Old Route 66. The closed building below states "No Place Like Texola".

Five

TEXAS

Route 66 traveled through the Texas panhandle for 178 miles. Today 150 of those miles are still drivable. Adrian, Texas has the distinct title of being the half way point between Chicago and Los Angeles. They have capitalized on being the Mid Point. See page 68.

This abandoned gas station on Route 66 is on the outskirts of Shamrock. The signs on the roof still advertise the world famous road.

The Tower Service Station was built in 1936 on the corner of Route 66 and US 83. At the far end of the restored building was the U-Drop Inn Restaurant. The building today houses the Visitor Information Center for Shamrock. Its likeness is featured in the Disney film Cars & Cars 2.

The Western Motel is across the street from the Tower Service Station seen on the opposite page. It is not fancy but neither are the rates.

This photograph shows yet another abandoned gas station. This one is in Lela. It appears at one time this was a very busy business.

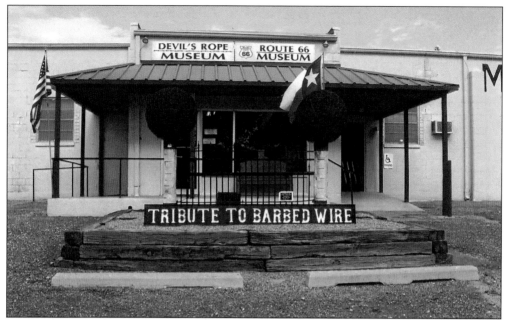

Barbed Wire, known as the Devil's Rope, was invented in 1868. Barbed Wire, as we know it today, was invented in 1874 by Joseph F. Glidden, known as the Father of Barbed Wire. This museum in McLean gives a complete education on barbed wire and its many related tools.

At one time many years ago this was the establishment to have your car repaired in McLean. This is the end result after falling into hard times.

This photograph shows the Cactus Inn in McLean. It was built in 1956 right on the side of Route 66 and still maintains the '50s look.

This is an old, hardly ever traveled, original unpaved alignment of Route 66 in the middle of nowhere between McLean and Britten.

This lone cow is the only living creature seen on this stretch of dirt road viewed on the previous page.

The eight states that Route 66 passes through are doing a great job of marking the way with these brown historical route signs.

There is no water, or never was, in the Britten leaning water tower. Ralph Britten bought it in the 1980s as an attraction to lure travelers off Interstate 40. He transported it from nearby Lefors to Groom and erected it at a tilt as it appears today. After stopping to take pictures, tourists would patronize his Leaning Tower Truck Stop for a bite to eat. Five years later the business succumbed to a fire and closed for good. The Leaning Tower of Texas, as it has been nick named, still attracts travelers for a quick photo.

This 190 feet cross is located on Interstate 40 at Groom, Texas. It was erected in July 1995 by the vision of Steve Thomas and his wife Bobby. The Thirteen Stations of the Cross encircle the base of it. There is also a Calvary Hill with the Three Crosses at the summit. It is breath taking.

This is the entrance to the building of the Cross Ministries. Besides the offices and Counseling Center there is a large gift shop. To learn more about the Cross Ministries visit **www.crossministries.net**.

This abandoned gas station and restaurant is on Route 66 between Groom and Adrien, the half way point of the journey.

Initially it was a small café with a dirt floor. From the late 30s to early 40s and into the 1950s it was known as Zella's Café. In 1956 it was sold and became Jesse's Café. An addition occurred and business was good until I-40 bypassed Rt. 66 and took the customers with it. It was sold again in 1976 to become Peggy's for 10 years before becoming Rachel's. After two fires and a remodel it was sold again in 1991. In 1995 the new owner discovered Adrian was midway between Chicago and Los Angeles, 1139 miles either way. He then changed the name from Adrian Café to "Midpoint Café and Gift Shop".

Six

NEW MEXICO

New Mexico Route 66 has one thing none of the other states have. They have the only Whiting Bros. Gas Station in existence in Moriarty. There once were over 100 of them throughout the western states. New Mexico also has a near complete 230 mile drive from Lupton to Moriarty.

The author, above, and John, below, are seen here talking to 83 year old Jack Gilmore and learned a lot about the area. He and his wife Pearl were married in the vicinity 66 years ago. Jack stops in most every morning for a cup of coffee and chats. This photograph was taken at the Tucumcari KOA campground. The owners also serve breakfast here, or you can take it out or call it in to be delivered right to your RV site.

This Hampton Inn at 3409 E. Route 66 Blvd. in Tucumcari was struck by lightning at 2:30 a.m. Wednesday morning July 16, 2014. It has been ruled a complete disaster. This photograph was taken August 9, 2014.

This Texaco station in Tucumcari has been restored. The Trade Station is now doing business inside. They buy, sell, and trade unique antiques, collectibles, jewelry, postcards, pottery, and more. It is very unique.

The author could not pass up recording this storm. Fortunately it was taking place a few miles south of Route 66.

The Palomino Motel in Tucumcari is a survivor. It was built in 1953 during the height of Route 66 travelers and is alive and well.

This Gulf gas station was built in the 1940s. But when Route 66 was widened they lost the gas pumps. However, with this concrete teepee attached to the front a new business was born and still survives today.

W.A. Huggins opened the Blue Swallow Court in 1940. Lillian Redman and her husband bought it in the 1950s and changed the name to Blue Swallow Motel. After more than 40 years, Ms Redman sold it in 1998. It has been fully restored to original condition and is still the icon it was.

There are over 100 murals painted on the sides of buildings in this town of Tucumcari. They were painted by former resident Doug Quarles.

In 1926 the Whiting Brothers constructed a profitable gas station using lumber from their fathers' mill. They grew the business to include cafés, motels and souvenir shops to their 100+ gas stations. The Whiting Bros. empire ended in the 1990s with only one station left in Moriarty, NM.

Pictured here is another Route 66 gas station that just could not survive after Interstate 40 was opened in 1981 and bypassed Tucumcari.

This 1950s Ford truck at one time had been converted into a very small camper. It appears it has been sitting beside Route 66 here in Tucumcari since before the Ranch House Café closed. It was opened in 1953.

This 1959 Edsel 4 door Ranger has been resting here since the sign looming above it advertised the Redwood Lodge, built in 1954.

Just outside of Tucumcari is this antique business. It was closed but very interesting. The headlight in the lower right corner is a tow truck. See opposite page.

This is the 1954 Chevrolet tow truck at this antique business. They have a little bit of everything. There was no sign advertising a name to the business. Below is a close up of the building seen above. Besides the old gas pumps, the Route 66 sign, and the Quaker State Oil sign, there is a sign over the entrance door that states American Owned.

Occasionally Route 66 comes to an end. This lonely section is between Tucumcari and Santa Rosa. This is part of the 15-20% of 66 not drivable.

The designers of Interstate 40 were considerate enough to provide this tunnel for Route 66 travelers to pass under the highway. It is just about large enough for a motor home to pass through.

This is the most unusual 1958 Edsel anywhere, period. It actually has an operational back hoe, see below. The controls, along with a seat, are mounted in the trunk. The controls for the bucket are located in the drivers' compartment. It is parked in front of the Route 66 Auto Museum in Santa Rosa. See next page.

This is the side of the Route 66 Auto Museum building seen on the previous page. Their business card reads: James "Bozo" and Anna Cordova and Children, Owners. "Bozo" restored all of the cars inside.

This is a beautifully restored 1963 Thunderbird convertible. It is slightly customized with spinner hub caps and a new grille. Note the painted bumper instead of the factory chrome. It also sports a tonneau cover.

This Mercury Montclair was the most popular model for the 1955 line up. The base price was $2,631. It is a really sharp looking car.

This sparkling Chrysler 300 came off the assembly line for 1966. It was their sporty leader and they all were equipped with front bucket seats.

This "AAA Approved" Ford tow truck sits proudly in front of the Route 66 Auto Museum. It also advertises "Bozo's Garage" on the door. The garage can be seen to the left center of the photograph.

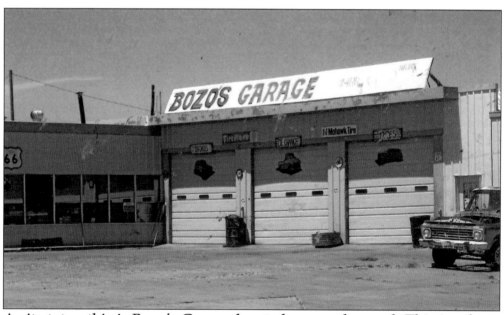

As it states, this is Bozo's Garage located across the road. This is where he restores the vehicles to place in his museum. By the way, Anna said Bozo drives each one of the cars occasionally.

The famous Blue Hole of Santa Rosa is a circular bell shaped pool, 240'
deep. It is one of the most popular scuba diving locations in the US. It is
a constant 64 degrees with a flow of 3,000 gallons of water a minute.

Club Café has been around since 1935. Ron Chavez, who passed away
October 15, 2014, saved it in the 1970s until he closed it in 1992. The
present owner has not been able to revive it and demolition is hovering.

In 1934, Roy Cline built a small Filling Station and Café at the corner of Highways 6 and 2 and named it Clines Corners. However, in 1937 when the highway moved a little north and became Route 66, he moved his business also. It has had five owners over the years and today Clines Corners Retail Center has over 30,000 sq. ft. of retail and restaurant. Below, the Mother Road travels down the Main Street of Albuquerque.

This photograph shows one of many motor courts along Route 66 that have survived. This one is the Cactus Inn Motel.

This old steel bridge used to carry Route 66 until the new road, left of the bridge, was built. Today I-40 to the right carries 99% of the traffic.

Above, is one lone house in the middle of nowhere. Below, the famous El Rancho Hotel in Gallup was built in 1937 by film director D.W. Griffith. It was a home for many Hollywood movie stars, from the 30s to the 50s, while filming westerns in the area. After I-40 opened, it declined. Armand Ortega bought and restored it. The slogan above the entrance announces; Charm of Yesterday – Convenience of Tomorrow.

The El Dorado Restaurant is located at 1805 W. Historic Highway 66 in Gallup. It appears to be closed.

This is one of many Sonic Drive-In Restaurants in the west. It is at 1901 W. Historic Highway 66 in Gallup.

Trains are alive and running in the west. Many trains have over 100 cars following four diesel locomotives. This BNSF Railway is the result of the Burlington Northern and Santa Fe railroads merging on September 22, 1995. The 390 railroads of the past combined over 160 years make up the BNSF. It now services the western two thirds of the U.S. This BNSF (above) is about to, and (below) is crossing Route 66.

Seven

ARIZONA

Only Arizona has the world famous Petrified Forest, the Painted Desert, and Meteor Crater. They also have the Twin Arrows, a Wigwam Motel, Jackrabbit Trading Post and above all else The Standin' On The Corner Park. The lovable Andy Devine called Kingman his home town.

The Petrified Forest National Park covers about 146 square miles. Route 66, BNSF Railway, and Interstate 40 all cross the park in an east to west direction. It was declared a National Monument in 1906 and a National Park in 1962. Over a half million people today, visit the park every year.

The Petrified Forest is known especially for its fallen trees, like the ones seen here. They lived about 225 million years ago.

It has been calculated the earliest human inhabitants arrived here about 8,000 years ago. About 600 archeological sites, including petroglyphs, have been discovered in the park.

This early 1900s automobile is resting along the side of road in the Petrified Forest. It represents the hard times of early travelers on Route 66. This park is the only National Park that Route 66 passes through.

Pictured here is a section of the Painted Desert. It has a total area of about 7,500 square miles or more than six times the size of Rhode Island (1,212 sq miles). The various colors come from the fine grained rock layers that contain abundant iron and manganese compounds.

This photograph gives a view of the Pow Wow Trading Post. It is located at 752 North Navajo Boulevard, Route 66 in Holbrook. They deal in Rocks (wholesale), Jewelry, Petrified Wood, and Clothing.

This is the front yard of Jim Gray's Petrified Wood Company in Holbrook. He buys petrified wood from all over the world. The picture below gives a good sampling of what he carries in his extremely large store. You can buy very tiny pieces to extremely large section of logs and everything in between. His website is **www.petrifiedwoodco.com**.

Pictured here is Wigwam Village Motel #6 in Holbrook. Architect Frank Redford built the first village in 1936 in Kentucky. There were 7 built between 1936 and the 1950s. Chester Lewis built this one in 1950. There are 15 concrete and steel teepees in a semi-circle around the office. He ran it until I-40 bypassed Holbrook in the late 70s and then sold it. After his death, his wife and children bought it, remodeled it, and reopened the business in 1988. Part of the office has been made into a museum.

Each teepee is 21 feet wide and 28 feet tall. They are all painted white with a fancy red band around the middle. Each one contains a bedroom and a bathroom with sink, toilet, and shower. Vintage automobiles are parked in front of each teepee, similar to this 1961 Ford Econoline. There are only two other villages left: #2 in Cave City, Kentuckey and #7 in Rialto/San Bernardino, California.

PONY EXPRESS

St. JOSEPH, MISSOURI to CALIFORNIA
in 10 days or less.

☞ WANTED ☜

YOUNG, SKINNY, WIRY FELLOWS

not over eighteen. Must be expert
riders, willing to risk death daily.
Orphans preferred.
Wages $25 per week.

APPLY, **PONY EXPRESS STABLES** ©
St. JOSEPH, MISSOURI   L. Macstas

The Pony Express was founded by William Russell, William Waddell, and Alexander Majors in 1860. The first westbound 2,000 mile trip rider left St. Joseph, Missouri on April 3, 1860, completing it in 9 days and 23 hours. Simultaneously, the eastbound rider left Sacramento, California and completed his ride in 11 days and 12 hours. The competition of the Pacific Telegraph sparked the end of the Pony Express on October 24, 1861, only 19 months later. At one time the Pony express had 100 stations, 80 riders, and 400-500 horses. They traveled 250 miles in a day. This advertisement tells clearly what breed of riders these men were.

Ten miles west of St. Joseph City is the Jackrabbit Trading Post, built by James Taylor in 1949. Famous signs along Route 66 kept stating it was only 90, 80, 70 etc. miles away until you reached this one. The trading post is on the road opposite the sign. A lesson in Advertising 101 can be learned. The Indian ruin below is in one of many Arizona Indian State Parks. This one is between Holbrook and Winslow.

Route 66 travels through Winslow but when I-40 bypassed the town in the 1970s, Winslow's businesses took a tail spin, many closing shop. It was not until September 1999 that it has been revived. This is when the "Standin' On The Corner Park" was dedicated, inspired by the group Eagles first single in 1972, "Take It Easy". The "On The Corner" gift shop, run by Don and Sandra Myers, is located below the sign above.

The two story wall seen here, behind a life size sculpture by Ron Adamson, is simply a free standing brick wall. The picture of the girl driving by in a flat bed Ford is a mural by John Pugh. The bricks in the park can be bought for 50, 100, and 250 dollars depending on the size. For more info or to buy a brick visit; www.standinonthecorner.com.

Meteor Crater is located 35 miles east of Flagstaff. The first written report of it was made in 1871 by a man named Franklin. The crater is 550 feet deep or equivalent to setting the Washington Monument (555 feet) on the floor of it. It is over 4,000 feet across and 2.4 miles in circumference. The visitor center complex is seen in the foreground. The embankment surrounding the crater rises 150 feet above the surrounding plateau.

The plaque reads: The Holsinger Meteorite is the largest discovered fragment of the 150 foot (45-meter) meteor that created Meteor Crater.

While at Meteor Crater John made friends with Gilbert (right), age 89, from San Jose, California. Gilbert was in Arizona visiting his brother Tony (left), age 87, from Tucson.

Twin Arrows is between Meteor Crater and Winona. It was built about 1950 and opened as the Canyon Padre Trading Post. Jean and William Troxell acquired it in 1954 and operated the business until 1985. However, it continued to stay open under new owners until 1998. It lay dormant until 2009 when the Hopi tribe and Route 66 fans restored the two arrows. The Hopi's plan to restore the store has not materialized.

This photograph was taken on August 11, 2014 and it appears the restoration never took place. The arrows, made from two telephone poles, look beautiful but the building is in very poor condition.

The Historic Seligman Sundries was built and opened in 1904. It has been home to a drug store with soda fountain, trading post, dance hall, and theater. It has been restored and again has a historic soda fountain.

Prescott Junction was founded in 1886. It was later renamed for Jesse Seligman. The town was booming, what with the railroad and Route 66. However, with the opening of I-40 in 1978 and the Santa Fe closing in 1985, Seligman's economy took a nose dive. Enter Angel Delgardillo, a barber, in 1987 was the driving force behind the creation of the Arizona Route 66 Association making Seligman the Birthplace of Historic Rt. 66.

Some of the signs on The Rusty Bolt are; Taxi Stand, Edsel Expressway, Beechwood 45789, and Lemon Cab Co. Seligman is a one of a kind stop.

The J & R Mini Mart pictured here advertises; Ice Cream, Espresso, and Groceries along with a Buffalo Burger, Fries, and a Can Soda for $8.00.

Angel's brother, Juan Delgardillo, built the Snow Cap Drive-In in 1953. To bring attention to his business he took the top off this 1936 Chevrolet and decorated it with horns, emblems and even a Christmas tree. Since Juan's death in 2004, his daughter Cecilia and son John operate it. Both brothers are acknowledged in the 2006 Disney/Pixar movie Cars.

Angel Delgadillo and Vilma Rampelotto were married in 1959. Angel began his barber shop business here in 1950 and later Vilma opened a gift shop. He has become known as the Guardian Angel of Route 66.

This early 1900s Ford pickup is at the edge of Seligman. Right now it is resting in some ones front yard. Yet, it appears to the author, it longs to join the Route 66 traffic going by, instead of slowly rusting away.

This is Seligman's Historic Route 66 Motel. They have 16 rooms and are AAA Approved. Rooms include Phone, Satellite TV, Refrigerator, Wi-Fi and Coffee Bar. The Road Kill Café's sign can be seen next door.

The Road Kill Café's menu lists; Deer Delectable's, Bad-Brake Steak, Fender Tenders, Caddie Grilled Patty, Splatter Platter, Swirl of Squirrel, Big Bagged Stag, and Highway Hash. Their motto is "You Kill It, We Grill It". It is a fun place to eat. To the right is the Historic Rt. 66 Motel.

This is the cover of the 31 page program for the Route 66 International Festival, held in Kingman, Arizona August 14-17, 2014. It was four days of jamb packed events from 8 a.m. to 10 p.m. There were VW and Classic Car Shows, Movies of Route 66, Concerts in Locomotive Park, Tours to the Diamond Distillery, Restaurants, and all kinds of Vendors selling Food or anything you could possibly want.

Part of the entertainment was "The Road Crew" pictured here. They are the official ambassadors for The Mother Road. "We spread the history and stories of Route 66 to every generation through our 'Songs From The Mother Road'. We encourage our audiences to discover America's Main Street for themselves." They continue; "We are dedicated to the preservation of the most famous highway in the world.....Route 66!" The card below was being given out at the Festival to anyone interested in listening to the great music of the 50s and 60s.

This colorfully dressed Indian dancer was part of a group that entertained on Saturday. Each costume is hand made by the dancer.

Adison (left) Miss C.R.R.U. Needles is posing for the camera with Gianna, Mrs. C.R.R.U. Needles. They are positioned on the stairs of an Atchison, Topeka & Santa Fe Railway locomotive in Locomotive Park.

John is conversing with the lady from the Lions Club. She and her two daughters are providing free bottled water to the visitors of the Festival.

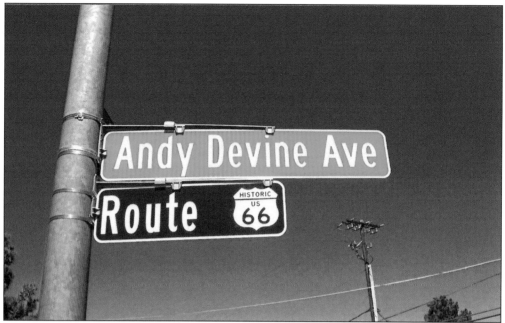

Andrew "Andy" Devine was born in Flagstaff, October 7, 1905. When he was one year old his father, Thomas Devine Jr., bought the Beale Hotel (below) in Kingman where Andy grew up. It is located at 325 E. Andy Devine Ave. and was successful for decades, first to the many passengers of the Santa Fe Railroad and then to travelers of Route 66. The main street, also Route 66, was renamed Andy Devine Ave. in 1955. He died February 18, 1977 at the age of 71.

Andy Devine was under contract with Universal Studios for fifteen years. He was Cookie Bullfincher in nine of Roy Rogers movies in the 1940s. He was the driver in the movie Stagecoach. Then he was Jingles P. Jones in the Wild Bill Hickok TV series in the 1950s. Also in the 1950s he hosted his own TV program, Andy's Gang. Andy Devine was second only to Walter Brennan for making more Class A movies as a western sidekick. In 1937, in Romeo and Juliet, he played Peter, the manservant. Andy also played in the original, *A Star Is Born*. In all, Andy made 400 films. (Leading Lights Autographs.)

The day was Saturday, the time was 1:00 p.m., the temperature was over 100 degrees, and the mode of transportation was on the back of a golf cart. This is a view of Andy Devine Avenue.

Still riding on the back of the golf cart, this is traveling down Beale Street on the way back to Locomotive Park.

John A. Dougherty, Kingman City Manager and his wife Ruth Anna were the great people that offered a ride on the back of their golf cart.

This 1959 4 door Edsel Ranger is just like the one on page 76, only fully restored. It was in one of the car shows. Having just driven under the Festival event banner, they are passing Locomotive Park on the left.

The Kingman Powerhouse was built in 1907 and generated power until 1938 when Hover Dam replaced it. By the 1980s it was in really bad shape, but thanks to the Powerhouse Gang it was saved and reopened in 1997 as the Powerhouse Visitor Center. These two photographs are an exhibit of people leaving the dust bowl area of the 1930s. The Arizona Route 66 Association and Gift Shop are also located here.

This exhibit demonstrates how the early settlers traveled across the prairie to build homesteads in the west. Everything they owned was in that wagon. There are more exhibits throughout the building.

The Detroit Electric was built from 1907 - 1939 by the Anderson Electric Car Company of Detroit. They built 13,000 of them. Top speed was about 20 mph and would go around 80 miles on a single charge. The Detroit Electric Holding Ltd. Co. of the Netherlands revived the brand in 2008 with Albert Lam, former CEO of the Lotus Engineering Group.

This business card tells you all about Rosie's Den Café. It is half way between Kingman and Las Vegas in the middle of nowhere. Below, on the wall is a framed photograph of Rosie. Pictured (L-R) is Rosie's daughter-in-law Sheila, Beth, and Sassie. Sassie is from Foxboro, Mass. and one day seven years ago she placed a U.S. map on the kitchen table, closed her eyes, and placed her finger on the map. She has been the bartender here since. Rosie has retired and her son Brad and Sheila now run the restaurant. News update: Rosie turned 89 on January 24, 2015.

A side trip to Hover Dam is well worth it. This view is looking north. The Hoover Dam contractors were given seven years to complete the project. They finished in five, 1931-1936. The new Mike O'Callaghan-Pat Tillman Memorial Bridge opened for traffic on October 16, 2010. The view below is looking south, taken from the top of the dam.

Hoover dam is in Black Canyon spanning the Colorado River between Arizona and Nevada. The dam is 726 feet tall; the towers go another 40 feet higher. Hoover Dam generates about 4 billion kilowatt-hours of hydroelectric power each year. They supply Arizona, Nevada, and part of California. Lake Meade, a byproduct of the dam, is down 140 feet in August of 2014. It has not been at the full line seen below since 1985.

This photograph shows if Lake Meade was at full capacity, this concrete spillway tunnel would be totally submerged.

This is a view of Route 66 leaving Kingman and headed to Sitgreaves Pass. This is a very picturesque, long stretch of road, going thru Mount Nutt Wilderness. This photograph was also used for the cover photo.

Cool Springs is at the entrance to the Black Mountains, on the winding road up to Sitgreaves Pass. It was built in the 1920s and soon had a café, a bar, and cabins. Route 66 bypassed it in 1953 and it was abandoned in 1964. In 2001 Ned Leuchtner bought it and completed restoration to original condition in 2004. However, there is no gas for sale here, only souvenirs. The old vehicles below sit along the side of the building.

While stopped at Cool Springs, the author met 86 years old Dan (above) and his wife Ruth 77 (below). They were traveling portions of Route 66, by motorcycles, on their way to visit their daughter in Colorado. The cool thing (pun intended) about it was they were from South County, Rhode Island. Plus another of their daughters lives in the same town as the author, Scituate, Rhode Island. What a coincidence.

The Pass is named for Captain Lorenzo Sitgreaves who was exploring rivers in the area in 1851. It is located west of Kingman on the first alignment of Route 66 in 1926. Vehicles without electric fuel pumps were reduced to backing up the pass. Fuel at the time was gravity fed.

Oatman, Arizona welcomes travelers coming from the pass and the hair pin turns of the mountain. It is definitely an extraordinary place to see.

Gold was first discovered in the area in 1902 by Ben Taddock. He sold his claim in 1903. In 1904 the Vivian Mining Company bought it and named the mining camp Vivian. From 1904 to 1907 the mine yielded over three million dollars. In 1909 the town changed the name to honor Olive Oatman. She was kidnapped by Apaches after massacring her family. It once boasted almost 4,000 people. Today about 100 people call it home year round. These photographs show you Main Street/Rt.66.

By 1930, it was estimated that 36 million dollars worth of gold had come from the Oatman and Gold Road mines. In 1952 Route 66 was rerouted to avoid Sitgreaves Pass which excluded Oatman. When the mines closed down the companies just turned their burrows loose and today as can be seen in these photographs they just roam the streets. In the late 1980s there was resurgence in traveling the old road. Then in 1995 the Gold Road mine reopened. Today Oatman is a tourist town.

Eight

CALIFORNIA

Route 66 in California lays claim to the end of the road at the Santa Monica Pier. After sitting on pins and needles crossing Sitgreaves Pass, the entrance to California is through Needles. Located in the Mojave Desert it is the hottest city on Route 66, also in the United States.

The steel truss railroad bridge can be seen on the opposite side (under) the bridge transporting Interstate 40 traffic. It is carrying 3 locomotives with 84 cars in tow. They are crossing the Colorado River heading east. This photograph was taken from the California side.

Upon entry into California, after crossing the Colorado River on Interstate 40 at Needles, this welcome sign alerts motorist to turn right at the next exit to continue their travels on Historic Route 66.

National Old Trails Road was established in 1912. It was 3,096 miles long, stretching from Baltimore, Maryland to Los Angeles, California. Much of US Route 66 followed this old trail through California.

The City of Needles is located in the Mojave Desert on the banks of the Colorado River in California. It took its name, in 1883, from the rock formation across the Colorado River in Arizona called The Needles.

The Route 66 Burger Hut Restaurant is located at 701 W. Broadway St. in Needles. This photograph was taken on August 19, 2014. Sadly, heavy winds damaged it in September 2014. The owners plan to rebuild the restaurant in the near future. It serves Mexican and American food.

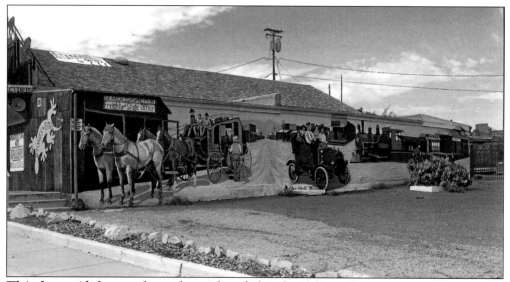

This beautiful mural on the side of this building depicts how the mode of transportation progressed to the west in the early days. First there was the stage coach and then came the train and finally the automobile.

The City of Needles has a number of murals throughout its streets. This one just simply advertises Route 66.

Yes, Betty Boop likes old cars and Route 66 also, as this mural indicates. Besides, she is helping to end; *Route 66 Today, Chicago, Il. to Needles, Ca.*

Images of America series
by Arcadia Publishing

The Lost Villages of Scituate: In 1915, the general assembly appointed the Providence Water Supply Board to condemn 14,800 acres of land in rural Scituate. The hardworking people of the five villages were devastated. By December 1916, notices were delivered to the villagers stating that the homes and land they had owned for generations were....

The Scituate Reservoir: In 1772, portions of Providence received water through a system of hollowed out logs. By 1869 the public voted in favor of introducing water into the city from the Pawtuxet River in Cranston. By 1900, it was clear more, and purer water was needed. A public law was approved on April 21, 1915, creating the Providence...

West Warwick: By 1912, the citizens of the western portion of Warwick had been talking about secession. They possessed all the mills on the Pawtuxet River and were largely democratic, while the eastern section was primarily republican. Finally in 1913, the town of West Warwick was incorporated and became the youngest town in the ......

Foster: Originally incorporated as part of Scituate in 1731, became a separate community in 1781. The town was named in honor of Theodore Foster, a coauthor of the bill of incorporation. By 1820, the population topped out at 2,900 and then sharply declined. The population would not surpass the 1820 figures until 1975.

Pawtuxet Valley Villages: Between 1806 and 1821, a dozen mills were built on the Pawtuxet River, shaping the economy of surrounding villages. The mills provided a livelihood for the villagers who settled in the valley and drew immigrants looking for a better life from Canada, Italy, Portugal, Sweden, and other faraway countries.

Coventry: On August 21, 1741, the area west of what is now the town of West Warwick was incorporated into the Township of Coventry. The railroad would traverse Coventry in the mid-1800s, providing the gristmills, sawmills, and farmers with a quicker way to send their goods to market and to receive supplies in return.

Gramma Larson Remembers series
by Wolf Publishing

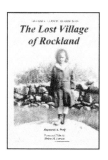

The Lost Village of Rockland is a book of photographs and documents with captions, featuring poems and tales by Helen O. Larson. She tells her story of growing up in the small New England Village of Rockland, in the Town of Scituate, Rhode Island in the early 1900s. She writes about having to suffer the agony of seeing her village vanish, one building at a...

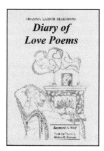

Diary of Love Poems is the second book of the *Gramma Larson Remembers* series. It is a story of a love that began on a bus in 1956. It continued until her husband Ivar passed away 32 years later. However, Helen's love for Ivar did not end then. It carried on for another 17 years until she left to meet him on.......

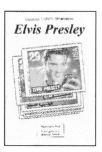

Elvis Presley is the third book in the *Gramma Larson Remembers* series. Her love for Elvis began in 1956 when she bought her son Raymond a portable record player with four 45 RPM records. One of the records was *Love Me Tender*. Through the years the boy born in a two room cottage in Tupelo, Mississippi rocked...

Famous People, Family and Friends is the fourth book in the *Gramma Larson Remembers* series. She wrote her first poem in the summer of 1923 at the age of twelve. In her later years she picked up the handle of being called Gramma Larson. During her 82 years of writing rhymes, she wrote about many things. This…

To order any of Ray's books visit:
www.raywolfbooks.com

About the Author

Raymond A. Wolf, with his wife Ramona, daughter Ashlee Rae, and Zoey the cat, lives in the Village of Hope, in the Town of Scituate, Rhode Island. He is a graduate of Scituate High School, retired from TJ Maxx, and belongs to six local historical societies.

In 1965 he traveled across the United States by automobile. Part of the trip was on Route 66. He drove across country again in 1986 but Route 66 had been decommissioned in 1985. Therefore, a lot of the trip was on Interstates. When he drove across again in 2005 parts of 66 was back. In the late 1990s to early 2000s there was resurgence in interest in the old road. Ever since then he has dreamed of driving the entire road.

After retiring in 2007 he started writing (nine) books, still talking about driving Route 66. So in 2014, the conversation between him and his wife Ramona, one morning over coffee, sounded like this:

Ray: "I sure would like to drive the entire length of Route 66."

Ramona: "You have been talking about it for seven years, why don't you just do it."

Ray: "Well you don't want to eat in diners and talk to old people, and that is what I want to do, plus I don't want to go alone."

Ramona: "So find someone to go with you."

Therefore, he and his friend John Donovan decided to do just that. Both Ramona and John's wife Mary said we deserved it and they would mind the home front while we were gone.

Today, you hold in your hands the results of that journey, *Route 66 Today – Chicago, Il. to Needles, Ca.*